Praise for *Diamond Grove Slave Tree*

"The legacy of George Washington Carver is an extremely
important component to the cultural heritage and identity of Iowa
State University. Xavier's unique and powerful voice has created
a compelling narrative that examines the struggles and triumphs
of the great scientist. With his voice Xavier has strengthened
the legacy of one of Iowa State's most storied alumni. Through
his narrative it is evident just how much that legacy has inspired
Xavier to create and succeed. As an educator for the University
Museums it is always thrilling for me when students on campus
today hear the stories of the past, find a resonant chord with
those who have come before, and harness that connection into
inspiration to create and succeed. Xavier has created a bold
and wonderful new reflection of the great scientist's life, and in
doing so, he has created a new and exciting outlet to engage with
and be inspired by the legacy of George Washington Carver."
—David Faux, Interpretation Specialist,
University Museums, Iowa State University

"Xavier Cavazos' portrait of George Washington Carver
creates a textured, nuanced look at this great Renaissance
man. Artist, musician, inventor, botanist, and one of the most
renowned scientists this country has ever known. Carver's life
was filled with struggles for racial equality. Through his highly
charged poetry, Cavazos slips into the skin of Carver and
humanizes this struggle, inviting the reader into the complex
world of a visionary agronomist. Cavazos makes a stunning
debut with this unique and powerful poetic biography."
—Mary Swander, Poet Laureate of Iowa

"Cavazos brings techniques of jazz improvisation to work bits and pieces of language into the edges and lesser-known undercurrents of the established melody of the life of George Washington Carver. 'O peanut/& sweet potato/Alabama & Georgia/hoe & sun,' Cavazos writes about the life and work of the famed African-American botanist and inventor who cultivated diverse crops such as peanuts, soybeans, and the sweet potato as alternative food sources for poor farmers, particularly in the South where cotton had depleted the soil of nutrients. Both the agricultural research and the biographical details of the life of Carver take on metaphorical significance in these poems, 'The goober and the yam/ready to reap riches/ from good Dixie soil.' This remarkable life, worthy of many biographies, has found one more gifted voice to praise and sing the complicated story of discipline and genius into the sunshine."
—Debra Marquart, author of *The Horizontal World: Growing Up Wild in the Middle of Nowhere*

"As Ralph Ellison would have it, a Yam is a Yam. And to Mr. Carver, a Peanut is More than a Shell. This book by Mr. Cavazos does justice to those ideas."
—Prof. Steve Cannon, *Gathering of the Tribes*

"*Diamond Grove Slave Tree* is where the Voice, the Academy, and History itself reweave a dancing formula. This is the book where Cavazos digs into poetry's forms and history's lessons, searing our eyes open with simple painful Truth-Art. It's an achievement and a gift. Read this book in silence, then shout Hallelujah—this is a new way of seeing."
—Bob Holman, Bowery Poetry Club, *Language Matters* PBS documentary

"This book is definitely meant to be read aloud to appreciate where Xavier is taking you. He captures your attention with a fresh but in-your-face perspective that forces you to look at the Carver experience all over again. To quote Carver 'it is the product of a creative mind.'"
—Thomas Moore, Executive Director,
African American Museum of Iowa

"In *Diamond Grove Slave Tree*, Xavier Cavazos forges a vision of story and song through history, examining a visionary in a kind of poetic totality that is populated by a galaxy of form and lyrical invention worthy of George Washington Carver's brilliance."
—Ryan Collins, Director Midwest Writing Center,
author, *A New American Field Guide &*
Song Book, (H_NGM_N Books)

"In this poetic biography about George Washington Carver, the author captures the essence of the human being beyond Carver as just 'the peanut man.' The reader—whether historian, linguist, student, teacher, rhetorician, or poet—is compelled to grapple with words as similes, metaphors, rhythms leap from the page, forcing a new (Re)construction of Mr. Carver. The author elicits details of Carver's life long forgotten, or ignored, by the historical record. Exiting the book, readers find themselves inquiring: Just who was George Washington Carver—ex-slave, 'peanut man,' scientist, genious, or world icon?"
—Dr. Bobby Cummings, Professor of English,
Director of Africana and Black Studies,
Central Washington University

DIAMOND GROVE SLAVE TREE

XAVIER CAVAZOS

For B!
how Awesom it is
to see you!! Many
blessings !

Ice Cube Press, LLC Est. 1993
North Liberty, Iowa

20/15

Diamond Grove Slave Tree
Copyright © 2015 Xavier Cavazos

Isbn 9781888160840

Library of Congress Control Number: 2014951492

Ice Cube Press, LLC (Est. 1993)
205 N. Front Street
North Liberty, Iowa 52317
319-594-6022
www.icecubepress.com
steve@icecubepress.com
twitter: @icecubepress

The paper used in this publication meets the minimum requirements of the American National Standard for Information Sciences— Permanence of Paper for Printed Library Materials, ANSI Z39.48-1992.

Manufactured in the United States of America.

Carver photo on cover and images inside book used by permission of the Special Collections Department / Iowa State University Library

Poetry Prize Editor: Elizabeth Macklin

"Without genuine love for humanity, it is impossible to accomplish much in this question of the races."
—George Washington Carver

Contents

III
For Victory and Peace

After
Marilyn Nelson

George Washington Carver
Overhears the Angels

Anagrams after Peter Pereira

In heaven the cherubim whisper
how words are morphing in hell.

To say *walk straight* to another demon
means *wag shirt & talk* aimlessly for awhile—

thinking his or her *talk was right* when really
not.   O those poor demons   busy running

around EARTH & hunger & how a *stolen harvest*
becomes the *haters solvent* & on this planet became *the slavers net*

& *hang the boy* was trumpeted as *began oh thy*
& O *heavenly father* became races' *fatal he her envy.*

O those busy demons burning down the lost birthday
cards of this world—all the I-love-you's & see-you-soons

of the mouth & body. The hungry human net
of trade & botany & bone-break—it is continuous—this *hunger*

& in hell the ghostly-white demons are *re-hung* daily
from a burning tree & *the burning tree* becomes *begin enter hurt.*

I

Plants as Modified by Man

Photos

The Polk Photograph

You are holding a bowl wooden &
carved-out the way your fingers look.

The wrinkles across your forehead, a migration of geese.
Or they are simply two lover birds

stretching their wings parallel in flight.
I wonder, George, what song you hear in your ear?

What musical process blooming like the flower
on your jacket? What scent released into air?

Clearly, you are in a laboratory at Tuskegee,
& wearing an apron like my mother would in the kitchen.

In the foreground, a sink faucet is blurred by the photo
& the faucet appears to be your walking stick.

There is something you are turning in the bowl.
Some discovery beginning to form &

light hits your nose down the ridge all gloss.
Behind you, everything is luminescent electric

from what must be an open window shade
& everything in the room, George, even the tone

of your skin, is luminous,
luminous, soft & light.

This Funny Photo

Hunched over
wearing a goofy

golfer's hat—
you are looking

for something
lost.   A golf ball perhaps

most likely though
you are picking

some budding
flower

some brilliant
bud

some tiny
plant

to s a v e

us

all.

A South

Soil & silt.

Loamy as black passage brown.

Crop this trade.

Eli 1794.

Lift chattel.

Pull & pluck.

Seed $ fiber.

Deposit

left

    &

P   A   R   A   D   E.

Virginia ports—
        cat-o'-nine-

tails.
    Knotted

           thongs

           cord.

Sunset

      plowed
cotton

roast   sun   row.
O

a slave.

O
O a brown

    lovely.
O.

O lovely
      this
          away
far

      home.

Boll Weevil

1

KING   cotton

                                       was

e-
       aten

by
       ME.

Was brought
to his

       knees
by tiny me.

Now
in

                         evening

                        I move

from tree

      to
weed

to   bankrupt
            billfold.

Funny
aren't

                    I
blackening

                    these
Southern fields?

                    This emptied
                                        space?

This

WHITE

L   a   n   d   ?

If
not
for
me
no
need
for
George
Washington

Carver.   No
alternative
crop
to
cotton.
No peanut

to crack
open.

No
shell
to
crunch.

Carver's National Lampoon Laboratory

O   Those white folks sure are funny ha-ha.
Funny like a cracked nut in a split open

shell.   Postured & more brittle than a dried
thistle in a closed bible-book.

Starch chemistry the way they marvel at me
like a colored comic—red & blue on my lip.

Hem-'n'-haw at my peas-in-a-pod.
Salted wounds heal quick

with reaction & blue ribbons
on the wall.   A phonograph plays

big-band classic in the lab.
Like a dog I smile & scratch

two glass beakers in my black-earth
hands.   So much electricity &

one wild-electrifying nut
coloring this whole tiny room.

The Nutritive Scale

Carver In Thought

A   slighter
                                           man

                                           radiates

heavenly

outward.
                                           A bug

                                           on a leaf

picked

     twig
     between

teeth.
                                           A tomato

                                           grows

& holds

     ripe juice
     on the vine.

                                           The tomato
                                           will grow

in any

                                           soil.

                                           Many

sizes

to garnish
fancy soup.

A light
loamy

mix

                              preferred

by

                              most.

                              More
                              yields

than   any other
                              peeled &

                              cut

                    L   A   R   G   E

Southern
red vine.

After George Washington Carver's "How to grow a tomato and 115 ways to prepare it for the table"

Root Cutting

July   best   to root
T   o   m   a   t   o

C   u   t   t   i   n   g   s.
Must   keep

Mo-
         ist.

Cutting
when the specimens

young   nice   roots.
                                                           Begin

bearing
as soon

as

          GROW
well.

                                        Preferred
over

premature
& older

                                                    stock.
Cutting t h e m

sooner
t h a n   l a t e r.

2

Stuffed Tomatoes

Select   onl(y)
fir(me)st.   Most

               developed!   Most
well-ripened

               of the bunch.   Re(move)
                               stem &

                               leaf.   Keep the
c(u)tting(s)

close.   Meat

                               chop

f(in)e
       (soil)   t   u   r   n

up
s(u)n.   Add

(crumb)s—a cup

of water

                               cooked

s(tic)ky-

                               skin

WARMING   A   DIRT   FLOOR.

Tomato (Spanish) Style

Peel   slice   (remove).
Cut

sm(all)

                                       p(i)eces.

                   ThreeThreeThree
                   ThreeThreeThree
                   ThreeThreeThree

bell peppers.

B(oil)   tender
two

                  levels of stacking.
T   o   o   l   o   n   g   !

Not   (moist)en   layer
                              oil
                    wrists   &

ankles.

                                                Cover the
                                                top

              while testing   the skin.
Bake one

                                                 hour.

Added

                                                   mixture

                                                   cooking

ti(me).

Tomatoes Broiled

The body
must be   wiped
                                                     clean.

Steri-   lized
any   connection

home.   Scald
the skin   with water

hot &   blistering
          as a   plague—

watch   beauty
leap   pulp

peel   cut
re-   strict

all   motion.
Place in   a bowl.

Calves   thick as
H   I   P   S.

A   pinch
of   pepper

to   remember.
Toast   quickly.

Until   brown
serve   hot.

Tomato Goulash

Can   everything.
Lean beef cut   &

kept   tight
large   sliced ones.

Even   small   strips.
Shredded   cabbage

the sound   of
language   pulled

A—   P—   A—   R—   T.   A heap
of   infant cry.

One   teaspoon
of salt   to freshen

the   wound.
A pinch   of foreign

vocabulary.   One cup
water   to keep

alive.   Add seasoning
for   fast work.

When finished pull
from heat   &

t   o   s   s

                        to the side.

Blossom-end Rot

| This | will end | the TOMATO. |
| All the | labor | for nothing. |

| Black | spots | beginning |
| at | the | blossom |

| end & | top. | CROPS |
| l | o | s | t |

foreverforeverforeverforeverforeverforeverforeverforeverfor—
foreverforeverforeverforeverforeverforeverforeverforeverfor—
foreverforeverforeverforeverforeverforeverforeverforeverfor—
foreverforeverforeverforeverforeverforeverforeverforeverfor—
foreverforeverforeverforeverforeverforeverforeverforeverfor—
foreverforeverforeverforeverforeverforeverforeverforeverfor—
foreverforeverforeverforeverforeverforeverforeverforeverfor—
foreverforeverforeverforeverforeverforeverforeverforeverfor—
foreverforeverforeverforeverforeverforeverforeverforeverfor—
foreverforeverforeverforeverforeverforeverforeverforeverfor—
foreverforeverforeverforeverforeverforeverforeverforeverfor—
foreverforeverforeverforeverforeverforeverforeverforeverfor—
foreverforeverforeverforeverforeverforeverforeverforeverfor—
foreverforeverforeverforeverforeverforeverforeverforeverfor—
foreverforeverforeverforeverforeverforeverforeverforeverfor—
foreverforeverforeverforeverforeverforeverforeverforeverfor—
foreverforeverforeverforeverforeverforeverforeverforeverfor—
foreverforeverforeverforeverforeverforeverforeverforeverfor—
foreverforeverforeverforeverforeverforeverforeverforeverfor—
foreverforeverforeverforeverforeverforeverforeverforeverfor—

foreverforeverforeverforeverforeverforeverforeverforeverfor—
foreverforeverforeverforeverforeverforeverforeverforeverfor—
foreverforeverforeverforeverforeverforeverforeverforeverfor—
foreverforeverforeverforeverforeverforeverforeverforeverfor—
foreverforeverforeverforeverforeverforeverforeverforeverfor—
foreverforeverforeverforeverforeverforeverforeverforeverfor—
foreverforeverforeverforeverforeverforeverforeverforeverfor—
foreverforeverforeverforeverforeverforeverforeverforeverfor—
foreverforeverforeverforeverforeverforeverforeverforeverfor—

the sky at night.

Biography of George Washington Carver
for Beginners

1

Diamond Grove, Missouri, 1864

Arrive a genius
of science.   No!

At Tuskegee Normal & Industrial
Institute for Training

Young Men & Women.
Not yet!   At Iowa State College

with Joseph Budd & Louis
Pammel.   Probably!

At Simpson College
in Iowa.   Yes!

At Highland Park University
in Kansas.   No never!

With art!   Yes!
Begin to learn

to read & write
with adopted parents

named Carver
& a birth brother

named Jim.   Hallelujah!
On a plantation

farm in Diamond Missouri.
A grove of walnut trees

shaped like a precious
stone.   Absolutely!

Arrive in Kansas
carried in the bag

of a slave raider.
O sweet Mary!

Stolen
with a raped

& murdered mother.
Merciful God!

With a dead father.
A slave at birth—

the dirt of Missouri mud.
Sweet Jesus!

Holy FATHER,
let all of this

now & forever
finally   yes

amen.

Slave

A seed in soil   dry &
brittle   lack of water.

In C
O
L
L
A
P
S
E
D
darkness
with sewer & sea on lip.

Shackled to a foreign language
the new O's wider than the rim

of   mouth
the round I   O   U nothing

of English bending   heart
beyond

                          recog(n)
                          ition

best   full sprint

(n)ot enough.

As you are
racked.

As you are   whipped.

As you are

                whispered your new

American name

                O lovely human

                yes
begin.

Diamond Grove Slave Tree

Witnessed by Young Carver

I see three
trees
wanting to
        s
              w
                    i
                          n
                                g

me.

Wild
trees
that look like
me.

Trees
three feet
wide &
full of HISTORY.

Trees
I should hide
from.

This
dangling
dark
branch
of a tree.

No!

Yes!
Never
fully
in
air.

II

A Résumé of the Period

Budd Family

The 1888 Experiment Station

Established by Joseph Budd

Fulfills the terms
of the Hatch Act of 1887.

Advances
science & solves problems

for the food
& natural-resource systems.

Links the plow, the seed,
imaginations of farmers & good folks

& in your case   George   breaks
boundaries of books & color.

Hal-le-lu-jah.
Was to glorify progress—

was to grow—
was to house—holler

was to add
was to—

was to—
was.

When Carver Sat Down in the Highland Park Methodist Episcopal Eating House

Morning   maybe   the
students   into   that.

Sun   the   hall
awoke   way.

One
whispered

to
be.

Students   white
the   ground

linen
fallen

rise   &
hang   before.

Colored   sit
us   our   one

student
rattling

tray   at   noon.

Collected Genera
from George Washington Carver

Cypripedium candidum

The blossom
droops

like a hung
head.

The
body

slender
& lean.

Root
dig-

ging
deep

into.

2

Juniperus virginiana

The Eastern
Red Cedar   clearly

the family shrub.
Bushy like a

mom.   Lots of
things

h
a
n
g
i
n
g
on

or around.
Leaves golden

& ROPE-like.
The sunk

face
of the flower

toward
the sun.

When Carver Sat Down in the Highland Park Methodist Episcopal Eating House

What   happened   here
inside   brick   college house?

Here,   lawns   fertile fields &
white snow   & dark   rich soil.

Here,   progress   sons &
daughters   segregated   South.

Here,   closing   door.
Kin I say.   Kind &   gentle.

Kin I say.   Sharp   rusty hoe.
What   hall   Carver?

Here,   student   rattled spoon

&   fork &   tray.
But George   did not   leave.

Here,   other   prominent
smiling   manner   yourself

during   environmental   experimentations,
during   mixing   minerals & books.

Here,   during   love.
Here,   during   truth.

H   E   R   E.

45

Collected Genera
from George Washington Carver

3

Erythronium americanum

                               Rich & shady
Dog Tooth Violets.

Long
stems

hold up the
moon with song.

Sways while you
sleep.   Sings

when you wake.
Dark bottoms

b   l   o   w   n
by wind

b-r-o-u-g-h-t
by ship.

4

Ranunculus septentrionalis

      The most WILD.
Best left t-i-e-d

in a group.
        Swamp

      Buttercups.
Love-morsels—

dark roots   unable
to untie.   One

bronze
bud   breaking

          b a c k
          S K Y.

When Carver Sat Down in the Highland Park Methodist Episcopal Eating House

Imagined

Maybe
eating house

good
Father's

porch
seeing

him
How else

grandfather &
Black

my heart.
Black girl

Woods.
father

flowers
given

I cried
nearly died

in family
this earth.

morning
I

whipping
rocking

between
boy

sitting
I love

his father
disgust

Hip
twelve &

Met there
caught

hand
picked

his face
night

in history
This one moment

that
being myself—

dad.
chair

hate
street

table with me.
a father

before?
grip

nice hip.
fourteen & alone

before my
us.   She was

I had
sun.

my father's
taught me

& beyond
forever

& now   a l l   I   d   o
exists &   black boy   sat

all   I   could   do   was   think of   my
father   what he   would do

to me   &   what he did
that   day   in   the   w   o   o   d   s.

Collected Genera
from George Washington Carver

5

Mertensia virginica

Woody
& dry.

Virginia

Bluebells

dominate the
vine.   Dead &

on paper the plant
s-i-l-h-o-u-e-t-t-e-s

a dark
hung bud

dotting
low

the
horizon.

The Hub

Progress

Just think   George
all that is left of the original

railway is just a few
rough roof trusses.

Not exactly the old station
that steam engines

screeched into.
Today   the building

serves lunch & Caribou coffee
snack treats   a place to cram

for a quiz
or meet a date.

No   not exactly the old
railway hub of 1891 to 1907.

Not exactly those
screeching tracks

that brought black
students from downtown

Ames to campus
to study at Iowa State.

No   not exactly those
dark iron rails.

No   not those same
black tracks.

No
not at all.

Staff Officers, 195, the *Bomb* yearbook

1895 *Bomb* Yearbook

Q-u-a-r-t-e-r-m-a-s-t-e-r
George Washington

Carver   you are standing
so erect in this student army

training corps photo.
Quartermaster—the highest rank

for any student—sealed & stamped
approval from the department

of Military Science & Tactics.
You are wearing two white gloves

& holding a cadets helmet
with an eagle emblem

on it.   Quartermaster
your uniform

the standard United States
officers fatigue.   Soaring

George   you are
                           Soaring.

Carver Dreaming

1898
Imagined

Dreamt I was one of the 10th Cavalry men—
black as an infantry gun barrel—

scarier than Roosevelt's Rough Riders
ripping up the plains—

barebacking the Comanche like
a spell   the Kiowa   the Kiowa-Apache

the Arapaho & Southern Cheyenne.
Dreamt I was a dark tropical soldier.

A real-live Spanish-regiment
fighter—bastard of the American

war.   1776's four score
& seven years

was never for us
the beloved 10th.

Like Geronimo
we keep fighting

on.   Dreamt I swam
to Cuba   took shelter under San Juan

Hill.   Ate tropical fruit.   Sewed
a blanket.   Killed a few Spanish soldiers.

Became a hero.
Prayed to my master

up in heaven.
I dreamt I was

a soldier.

Letter to Booker T. Washington

Ramer, Alabama, 1902

The night train to Ramer
was not a pleasant

experience. I travelled
with a wonderful

photographer. A white
woman friend, well-dressed

& spoken. The station folks,
hotter than the box train

we rode in. We sat
side by side. She

no more interested
in me, than I, in her.

I've done much
by way of better crops

for white farmers?
But even here in Ramer,

at night
I dream of the rope,

the tree
& the large

gathered
crowd.

III

For Victory and Peace

This Labor

Carver In Thought
For Austin W. Curtis, Jr., Carver's Love
Imagined

1

                        Father
your finger   heavy

on my heart.
S   o   m   u   c   h

isolation   even
I dream of the

Consum(mate).   But
my thoughts are more

dangerous than eating
with a white man

in Alabama
in Birmingham.   The class-

room   Lord   all I have—

marvel

& amazement—
his tight skin

                        O
                        father

this young
boy.

There is a line
            Father,

people are not wanting
to cross.   Color must

chose sides.
            But   Lord,

I cannot lie,
these things

weigh not down on me.
            For me, Lord,

Master,
the question

is a matter of the firm
grip of hand—

a gentleman's
squeeze.

How do I
indulge the spirit?

He is so tall &
in the room.

My Austin,
O

the sparkling
lustful eye.

3

Have I not   brought you enough plants,
many specimens   to choose from?

The sun,   an open
mouth.   My offerings, the tilted

leaves I bring.   I pour
everything I have   into

night & day.   The wild dream.
The drained body

                     before sunrise. The
growth between shine

                     & leg.
A black sky hears my

                     thoughts &
prayers.

                     My desire, Lord,
& the one

                     impossible
wish.

4

                              Tell me   Lord.
Tell me where to lay my head

at night   the owl hoots &
calls me friend.

I can no longer see a difference
in specimens, the handling

of such things.   Black &
white.   Boy & boy.

Stem or leaf.
Who, who, who shall feather

D
O
W
N
with me at evening time?
                         You   Lord,

You?

"The Goober and Yam to Enrich the South,"
Carver Writes

The goober & the yam
ready to reap riches
from good Dixie soil.

Tapioca & starch
ready to make the yam
famous as money.

O peanut
& sweet potato
Alabama & Georgia

hoe & sun. O
how a field will feed
a belly full.

                O how
a full belly
wants a soul empty

working a row
of fields of goober & yam
O how the empty soul dies.

Photos

3

Statue of Carver, National Monument
Diamond Grove, Missouri

You are sitting on a rock
      naked from the waist up.

Your chest blending in amongst
      tree & leaf the sun hits.

The shadow in this photo
      has hidden your young face

but you are looking up to God
      your only Christ & savior.

Missouri trees have formed a shelter
      around you while you think about

your missing mother
      while you daydream about plants &

birds & for this one glorious moment
      imagine this earth this heavy rotating

rock in space has forgotten about whip
      & chain & dog & hoe &

in this one record
      of time   celebrates your genius

&

      birth.

The Death of
George Washington Carver

January 5, 1943

They had it right, George
the history books & all.

They had it right, O
lowly sweet potato—

O lowly peanut red clay—
O lowly African slave—

wild & fruitful as a nut & grease—
tree & rope working

gangly like figs.
        F.D.R. said it best:

"It was a loss to mankind."
      You developed like gas & star.

           You, the root,
           you, the tree,
           you,
           you,
           O
           you!

Just Thought You'd Like to Know,
Mr. Carver

1

That there is a thirty-two-cent
stamp of you   out there

somewhere   right now—
with a sweet potato

& peanut plant right
behind a microscope—

with your name typed
beautifully along the right

side of the edge & you
are grinning   George

grinning like you just won
a great big hand of poker—

grinning like a wild big bet
& the United States

of America   good Old Glory
herself   has put all of her

authority   all of her amazing
grace   everything all

gloriously
around you.

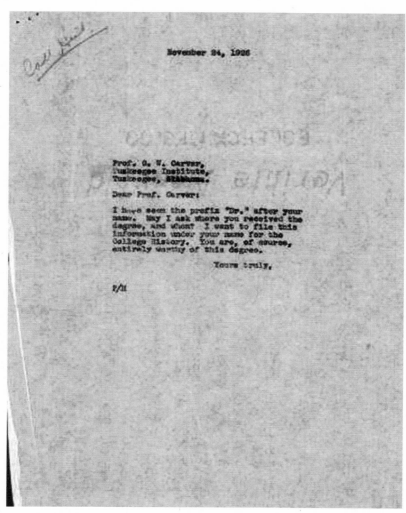

November 24, 1926

Prof. G. W. Carver,
Tuskeegee Institute,
Tuskeegee, Alabama.

Dear Prof. Carver:

I have seen the prefix "Dr." after your
name. May I ask where you received the
degree, and whent I want to file this
information under your name for the
College History. You are, of course,
entirely worthy of this degree.

Yours truly,

P/M

Letter From Pammel to Carver, November 24th, 1926

69

That on the fourteenth
day of May   in the year

one thousand
nine hundred & ninety-four

the Iowa State University
of Science & Technology   hereby

bestowed upon you the honorary
degree of DOCTOR

of Humane Letters—
with all the honors &

distinctions belonging to this
one degree with the signatures

of the president of the state
board of regents

& president of the university
with one solid sealed

stamp & no misspelled
words & in a very nice framed

case.   Well   I just thought you'd
like to know   George

no misspelled words &
in a very nice framed case.

3

That your alma mater
your old Iowa State

                                        was the first & is the only
                                        division-one school

to have a huge football
field named after its first African-

                                        American
                                        athlete.   Now   George

of course I know
you were the first

                                        African-American
                                        student here in 1891

but Johnny-Jack
Trice is the first African-American

                                        to have a gigantic
                                        stadium

in the Big-Twelve
Conference

                                        or anywhere for that matter
                                        named after him.

I know you knew
he died

                                                    in 1923
                                                    in his first football game

against Minnesota
when the refs let the team

                                                    gang-pile
                                                    on him & collapsed

his lungs
like the   t   o   w   e   r   s

                                                    but   I wanted
                                                    to let you know

about the 56,795-seat
JACK TRICE STADIUM

                                                    which came after you.
                                                    I wanted to let you know

what your alma mater
has been up to—

                                                    what your old
                                                    nourishing mother

& her students
have done.

Photos

4

Black & white

Older &
in the South

        you are framed
        by a white

border   not
a white lynch

        mob
        like yesterday's

newspaper
heading

        where a young
        man was tied

to a tree
for speaking

        to a white girl.
        All of this   George

more than one hundred
& fifty years after

        the Declaration
        of Independence.

All of this   thirty
years before

                    Martin Luther King, Jr's
                    letter to eight Alabama

clergymen.
Your mustache

                    & hair the color
                    of salt & pepper

spilt on the dinner
table   but you are eating

                    & certainly at a table.
                    I can tell by the look

on your face   George
that this news saddens

                    you   but somehow   some-
                    amazing-miraculous-how

your scientific eyes
are gazing

                    beyond race
                    & tree hangings

beyond the South
& soil

                    beyond salvation
                    & the eternal grave

some-amazing-
how   George

        beyond all of this
        American

messy .... thing.

A Prayer

                              Bless the sea
                              crossed
to get from fauna
to famine.

         Fancy clasps
for the feet.   Fairy

tales   & dreams moist
as a slave-ship sail.

Bless the highs & lows—
                   the lost ones

                   the loved ones
holding

         down

the sea.   This day
                   is for you

                   the
                   exalted

                   & sunk
                   language

that is   A   L   L   U   S
               the forgotten father

the beloved
mother tongue.

Special Thanks:

Diamond Grove Slave Tree, would not be possible without the support of Ice Cube Press and Midwest book publisher
Steve Semken: Many Blessings!

My endeared close readers
to whom I owe a lifetime of literary blessings!
Jim Hanlen
A. Van Jordan
Steve Pett
Mary Swander
Debra Marquart
Katharine Whitcomb

All my praise to the 2014
Prairie Seed Poetry Prize Editor:
Elizabeth Macklin

Additional copy editing support:
Darik Brown, Steven Castro Jr, Donson Curtiss,
Casey Friedman, Zachary Harris, Daniel Haskin,
Kendra Hinger, Olivia Hirschey, Alisa Hoag,
Karie May, Ebonesiah Morrow, Daisy Perez, &
Ashley Schuknecht

I'd also like to thank the entire faculty of Iowa State University's
MFA in Creative Writing & the Environment program, where all
the writing of this book occurred.

Special thanks to Iowa State University's
Parks Library Special Collections for allowing me time with their
archived George Washington Carver collection.

Deborah Lewis and the Ada Hayden Herbarium
for allowing me time with their Carver Collection.

Iowa State University Museums &
University Museums Interpretation Specialist David Faux.

For all my Family:
Cavazos, Cerna, Flores, Jaramillo, Kilpatrick.

And finally to my world:
Shelly, Dominic, Brooklyn and Carlos!
I can't image a life without you.

Acknowledgments

"Photos," appeared as, "The Polk Photograph of George Washington Carver," *Crab Orchard Review*. Vol. 16, #2.

"Biography of George Washington Carver for Beginners," *Tribes 14*.

"Boll Weevil," "Collected Genus Species by George Washington Carver for Dr. Louis Pammel, Caver's Mentor & Professor," "1895 Bomb Yearbook," "Carver Dreaming 1898," appeared in *Prairie Gold: An Anthology of the American Heartland.*

"Just Thought You'd like to Know, Mr. Carver," *Colbalt Reading Series #400*

Nine poems from this book were named a Runner-Up Prize in the 2011 Unterberg Poetry Center's 92nd Street Y "Discovery" *Boston Review* poetry contest. The judges were Cornelius Eady, Brenda Hillman, & D.A. Powell. I would like to extend grateful acknowledgment to the judges and the editors.

Xavier Cavazos is the author of *Barbarian at the Gate*, selected and introduced by Thomas Sayers Ellis as part of the Poetry Society of America's New American Poets Chapbook Series. *Diamond Grove Slave Tree* is the inaugural Prairie Seed Poetry Prize from Ice Cube Press. Cavazos teaches in the Central Washington Writing Project, Africana and Black Studies, and the Professional and Creative Writing Programs at Central Washington University.

The Ice Cube Press *Prairie Seed Poetry Prize*
celebrates the use of poetry to explore and better understand
the history, people, culture, folklore, and themes of living in
the United States Heartland.

Check our website beginning April 2015 to learn about
entering out 2015 prize at
http://www.icecubepress.com/poetry-prize

The Ice Cube Press began publishing in 1993
to focus on how to live with the natural world
and to better understand how people can best
live together in the communities they share and
inhabit. Using the literary arts to explore life and
experiences in the heartland of the United States we
have been recognized by a number of well-known
writers including: Gary Snyder, Gene Logsdon,
Wes Jackson, Patricia Hampl, Greg Brown, Jim
Harrison, Annie Dillard, Ken Burns, Roz Chast,
Jane Hamilton, Daniel Menaker, Kathleen Norris,
Janisse Ray, Craig Lesley, Alison Deming, Harriet
Lerner, Richard Rhodes, Michael Pollan, David Abram, David Orr,
and Barry Lopez. We've published a number of well-known authors
including: Mary Swander, Jim Heynen, Mary Pipher, Bill Holm,
Connie Mutel, John T. Price, Carol Bly, Marvin Bell, Debra Marquart,
Ted Kooser, Stephanie Mills, Bill McKibben, Craig Lesley, Elizabeth
McCracken, Dean Bakopoulos, and Paul Gruchow. Check out Ice
Cube Press books on our web site, join our facebook group, follow us on
twitter, visit booksellers, museum shops, or any place you can find good
books and discover why we continue striving to, "hear the other side."

Ice Cube Press, LLC (est. 1993)
205 N. Front Street
North Liberty, Iowa 52317-9302
steve@icecubepress.com
twitter @icecubepress
www.icecubepress.com

to Laura Lee & Fenna Marie
superb & shining
way beyond diamonds